Electronic Warfare: Radar Jammer Proliferation Continues: NSIAD-92-83

U.S. Government Accountability Office (GAO)

The BiblioGov Project is an effort to expand awareness of the public documents and records of the U.S. Government via print publications. In broadening the public understanding of government and its work, an enlightened democracy can grow and prosper. Ranging from historic Congressional Bills to the most recent Budget of the United States Government, the BiblioGov Project spans a wealth of government information. These works are now made available through an environmentally friendly, print-on-demand basis, using only what is necessary to meet the required demands of an interested public. We invite you to learn of the records of the U.S. Government, heightening the knowledge and debate that can lead from such publications.

Included are the following Collections:

Budget of The United States Government
Presidential Documents
United States Code
Education Reports from ERIC
GAO Reports
History of Bills
House Rules and Manual
Public and Private Laws

Code of Federal Regulations
Congressional Documents
Economic Indicators
Federal Register
Government Manuals
House Journal
Privacy act Issuances
Statutes at Large

United States General Accounting Office

GAO

Report to the Chairman, Committee on
Armed Services, House of Representatives

February 1992

ELECTRONIC WARFARE

Radar Jammer Proliferation Continues

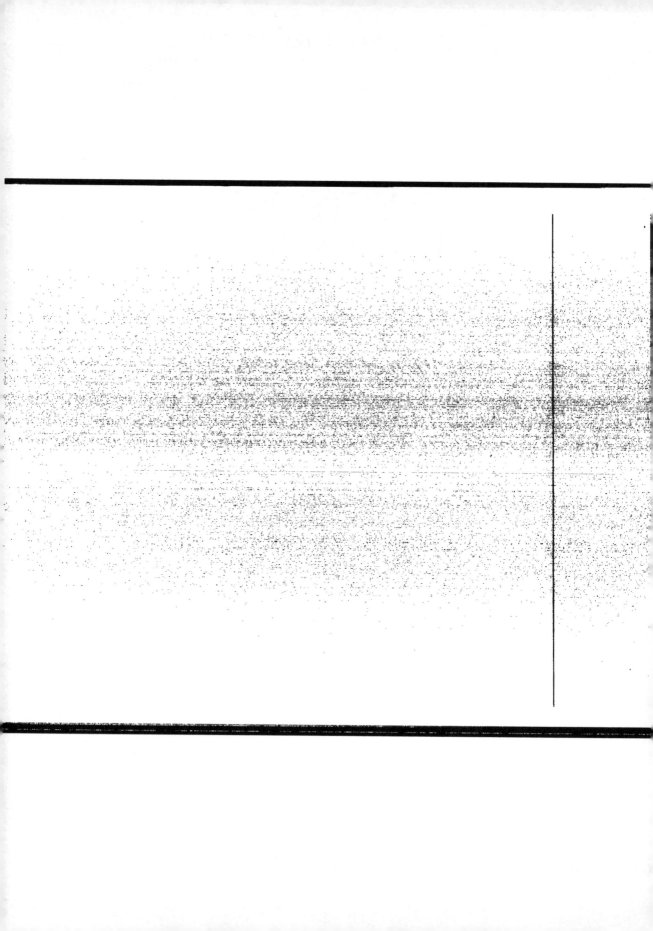

United States
General Accounting Office
Washington, D.C. 20548

146082

National Security and
International Affairs Division

B-243199

February 28, 1992

The Honorable Les Aspin
Chairman, Committee on Armed Services
House of Representatives

Dear Mr. Chairman:

This report, which was prepared at your request, assesses whether Navy and Air Force radar jammer programs are consistent with the congressional goal of reducing the proliferation of electronic warfare systems.

We plan no further distribution of this report until 10 days from its issue date. At that time, we will send copies to the Chairmen, Senate Committee on Armed Services and Senate and House Committees on Appropriations; the Secretaries of Defense, the Air Force, and the Navy; and the Director, Office of Management and Budget.

This report was prepared under the direction of Mr. Louis J. Rodrigues, Director, Command, Control, Communications, and Intelligence Issues, who may be reached on (202) 275-4841 if you or your staff have any questions. Other major contributors are listed in appendix II.

Sincerely yours,

Frank C. Conahan

Frank C. Conahan
Assistant Comptroller General

Executive Summary

Purpose

The military services have spent more than $9 billion on electronic warfare devices called jammers to protect tactical aircraft against threat weapon systems. Jammers protect aircraft by transmitting electronic signals to interfere with the radars used to control threat weapons.

Statutory requirements and congressional committee comments repeatedly encouraged the services to develop electronic warfare systems that can be used by more than one service to meet the common air defense threat. Achieving commonality among the services avoids duplicative costs for system development, enables lower unit production costs through larger quantity buys, and simplifies logistical support while reducing costs.

At the request of the Chairman of the House Committee on Armed Services, GAO assessed whether Navy and Air Force jammer programs were consistent with the congressional goal of reducing the proliferation of electronic warfare systems. GAO focused on those jammers intended to protect tactical fixed wing fighter and attack aircraft. GAO's work excluded any jammers that could be under development for future generation aircraft.

Background

In 1985, GAO reported that the Air Force had not taken advantage of the opportunity to reduce proliferation of electronic combat systems as intended by various congressional committees. GAO recommended measures intended to promote commonality in Air Force and Navy systems.

The Department of Defense (DOD) disagreed with GAO's recommendation. However, DOD commented that it was committed to achieving commonality and that a statutorily mandated electronic warfare master plan was being developed that would provide the best road map to commonality. Further, DOD stated that ongoing efforts were expected to achieve 50 percent commonality over the next 10 years.

Results in Brief

Despite statutory and committee report emphasis and DOD's stated commitment to commonality, the military services have continued to acquire numerous, different jammer systems to protect the same type of aircraft against a common threat, and no commonality has been achieved. Further, since GAO's 1985 report, the prospects for achieving commonality have deteriorated because the Air Force abandoned the only program having promise for commonality.

The proliferation continues in large part because DOD has not been effective in overseeing the services' jammer programs. In addition, DOD has not developed an effective electronic warfare master plan to achieve the intended commonality.

Principal Findings

Services Continue to Proliferate Costly Jammer Systems

Rather than promote the use of a common jammer, the Air Force and the Navy are using or acquiring 12 different self-protection jammers and two separate mission support jammers to protect tactical aircraft against a common threat. These jammer systems represent an investment exceeding $9 billion, and none are common to both Air Force and Navy aircraft. In addition, the Air Force has procured different jammer systems, such as the ALQ-131 Block II and the ALQ-184, to protect the same aircraft. In 1989, after acquiring over 600 of these jammers, the Air Force selected the ALQ-184 to meet its future needs but still has requirements to continue upgrading both jammers.

Prospects for Commonality Have Deteriorated

At the time of GAO's 1985 report, the Airborne Self-Protection Jammer (ASPJ) was designated by DOD to be the common jammer for Air Force and Navy aircraft, saving an estimated $1.2 billion. However, the expected commonality has not been realized. First, after reducing the types of aircraft to use ASPJ, the Air Force began developing a new jammer, the ALQ-189, for an aircraft that could use ASPJ. The Air Force later abandoned the ALQ-189 after spending $87 million on its development. Then, in 1990, the Air Force withdrew from the ASPJ program, citing poor test results, congressional restrictions on production, and high cost as the reasons. The withdrawal significantly reduced the number of ASPJ units to be procured, and contributed toward an increase in its estimated unit cost from $1.4 million to $2.3 million. The Air Force still has a requirement for a jammer like ASPJ.

The Air Force and the Navy are also separately upgrading the ALQ-99 mission support jammer, and the upgrades will increase proliferation. The Navy is spending an estimated $1.3 billion, while the Air Force is spending $726 million to upgrade different components of the jammers.

DOD Lacks Adequate Control Over Service Programs

DOD has not effectively exercised oversight over jammer upgrade programs, resulting in jammer proliferation. For example, while ASPJ was under development, and without any approval by DOD, the Air Force began two upgrades of its ALQ-135 jammer at an estimated cost exceeding $2.1 billion. With the upgrades, the ALQ-135 is expected to have capabilities very similar to ASPJ. A comparison of the jammers when the decisions about the upgrades were made could have resulted in a single common system.

In addition, DOD has developed the congressionally mandated electronic warfare master plan, but not so that it can be used as a road map to commonality. The plan represents little more than listings of systems that the services plan to acquire or upgrade and contains no provisions for achieving commonality.

Recommendations

If the continued proliferation of jammers is to be curtailed, a stronger role by DOD appears essential. GAO therefore recommends that the Secretary of Defense perform an analysis to determine the most cost-effective self-protection jammer for maximum common use on existing Air Force and Navy tactical aircraft. This analysis should weigh each jammer against all other jammers to identify the jammer that provides the highest level of aircraft protection for the funds invested. Costs considered in the analysis should include all future costs applicable to each jammer's life cycle. After the best jammer is selected, DOD could restructure the electronic warfare master plan to prescribe guidance, including timetables, for installing the jammer on the maximum practical number of Air Force and Navy aircraft. This approach should minimize upgrading of the numerous existing jammers.

GAO also recommends that the Secretary establish controls over the services' jammer programs, such as DOD review and approval authority, to achieve commonality whenever feasible.

In addition, GAO recommends that the Secretary require the Air Force and the Navy to merge the separate ALQ-99 upgrade programs to improve commonality.

Matters for Congressional Consideration

Despite long-standing committee emphasis and more recent legislation aimed at promoting commonality, none has been achieved. The potential for commonality that existed in the mid-1980s has since deteriorated. Thus, Congress may want to

- restrict or deny funds to procure new systems or upgrade existing jammers until DOD has done an acceptable analysis consistent with GAO's recommendation to the Secretary of Defense and then fund only those programs that are consistent with the analysis and
- require DOD to establish a joint jammer program office and centrally control all jammer funding to promote commonality.

Congress may also want to monitor programs for future generation aircraft to assure that they do not lead to further proliferation.

Agency Comments and GAO Evaluation

DOD partially agreed with the findings in this report. However, it disagreed with certain of the report's recommendations and stated that the remaining recommendations had already been accomplished.

DOD said that it had completed the recommended cost-effectiveness analysis as part of a congressionally directed review of electronic warfare programs. However, the analysis done by DOD was not the type called for by GAO's recommendation because it did not attempt to determine the most cost-effective jammer for maximum common use.

DOD also stated that the recommended controls over the services' jammer programs already exist. While controls cited by DOD do exist, GAO believes that this report demonstrates that they have not been effective in achieving commonality.

DOD disagreed with GAO's recommendation to merge the separate ALQ-99 upgrade programs. DOD cited an agreement between the Air Force and the Navy to cooperate in developing the upgrades. However, GAO is concerned that the remaining commonality will further deteriorate under these separately managed programs.

Contents

Abbreviations

ASPJ   Airborne Self-Protection Jammer
DOD   Department of Defense
GAO   General Accounting Office

Introduction

The potential threat to tactical aircraft includes both land-based weapons, such as surface-to-air missiles, as well as weapons launched from hostile aircraft. Many of these threat systems rely on radars to detect and track target aircraft and, in some cases, to guide the missile to the target or direct gunfire.

To protect aircraft from these threats, the military services equip them with electronic warfare devices called radar jammers. As figure 1.1 shows, jammers protect aircraft by sending signals that interfere with the radar fire control and guidance systems of enemy weapons. The military services consider jammers to be critical to the survival of tactical aircraft for all projected wartime missions.

The services use two types of jammers referred to as self-protection and mission support. Self-protection jammers are carried on attack aircraft, while mission support jammers are carried on electronic warfare aircraft to provide additional electronic countermeasures support for attacking aircraft.

Four major self-protection systems that are being acquired or have upgrades pending are the Navy's Airborne Self-Protection Jammer (ASPJ) and the Air Force's ALQ-135, ALQ-131, and ALQ-184. The ASPJ and ALQ-135 are both mounted inside the aircraft, while the ALQ-131 and the ALQ-184 are mounted underneath the aircraft fuselage or wing in pods. ASPJ was also being developed in a pod configuration; however, that effort was recently terminated. The ALQ-99 is a mission support jammer used on the Navy's EA-6B and the Air Force's EF-111A electronic warfare aircraft. These jammer systems are in varying stages of development, production, and/or upgrade and are shown in figures 1.2 through 1.6.

Figure 1.1: Effects of Jamming

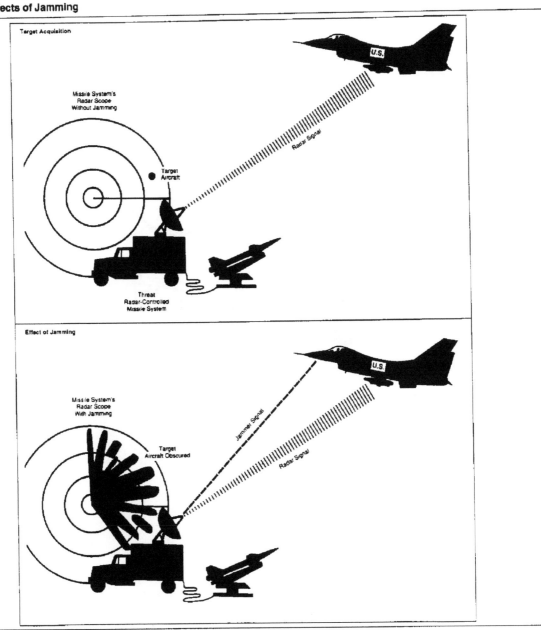

Source: GAO Artist's Rendering

Figure 1.2.: Airborne Self-Protection Jammer

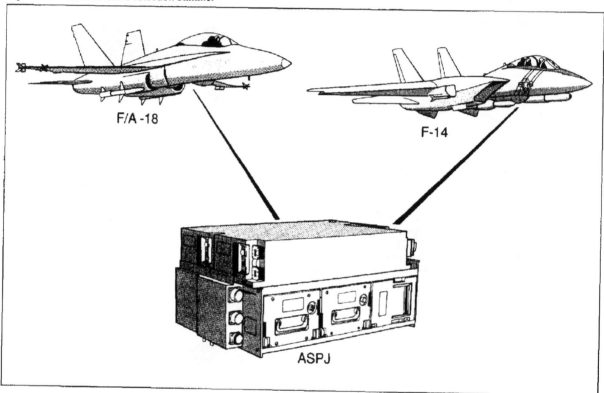

Source: GAO Artist's Rendering

Figure 1.3: ALQ-135 Preplanned Product Improvement

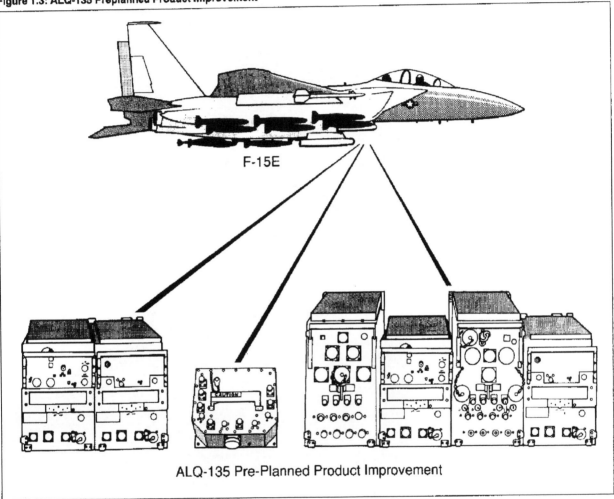

ALQ-135 Pre-Planned Product Improvement

Source: GAO Artist's Rendering

Figure 1.4: ALQ-131 Block II

Source: U.S. Air Force

Figure 1.5: ALQ-184

Source: U.S. Air Force

Figure 1.6: Air Force Version of ALQ-99

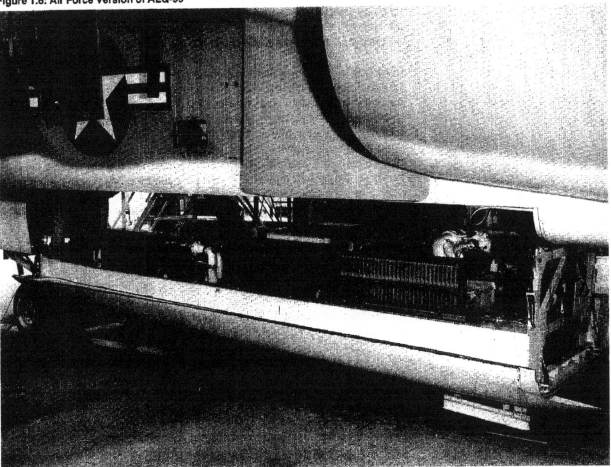

Source: U.S. Air Force

Prior GAO Work

In 1985, we reported that the Air Force had not taken advantage of the opportunity to reduce jammer proliferation by pursuing the use of the jointly developed ASPJ. Instead, the Air Force had decreased its planned use of ASPJ and was developing upgraded versions of other jammers, such as the ALQ-131, to meet a common threat.

We recommended that the Secretary of Defense require an independent assessment of the ALQ-131 and ASPJ programs to include their relative cost and performance capabilities as well as consideration of other jammer upgrade programs. We further recommended that after completing the assessment, the most cost beneficial system should be developed in pod and internal versions to satisfy interservice requirements.

In response, the Department of Defense (DOD) recognized both the economic savings and operational benefits that could be derived from using a common jammer. However, DOD did not concur with the recommendation, stating it had already evaluated these jammers, and based on those evaluations, it was not possible to satisfy current or short-term requirements with a single jammer in pod and internal versions. According to DOD, significant commonality was not possible immediately; however, ongoing efforts were expected to achieve 50 percent commonality over the next 10 years. Further, DOD stated it was developing a statutorily mandated electronic warfare master plan that would provide the best road map to commonality.

Objective, Scope, and Methodology

At the request of the Chairman, House Committee on Armed Services, we evaluated the services' radar jammer acquisition and upgrade programs to determine if they were consistent with the statutory goal of reducing the proliferation of electronic warfare systems. We concentrated on those jammers used to protect Navy and Air Force tactical fixed wing fighter and attack aircraft.

We did not examine Army jammers because commonality between fixed wing fighter aircraft and helicopters used by the Army was impractical due to differing weight and power requirements. Similarly, we excluded jammers for deployed strategic bombers because differing requirements precluded commonality. In addition, we did not include any self-protection jammers that may be under development for advanced Air Force and Navy fighter and attack aircraft.

Additionally, the Committee staff asked us to evaluate DOD's response to provisions of the Fiscal Year 1991 National Defense Authorization Act requiring establishment of a joint, cost-effective electronic warfare modernization program. The act stipulated that the modernization program meet essential operational requirements, eliminate redundancy, and maximize commonality among specified jammer programs, including ASPJ, ALQ-135, and ALQ-184. However, as agreed with the Committee staff, we are reporting on this issue separately.

In evaluating the proliferation of jammers, we reviewed system acquisition plans, documents that outlined the program justification and system needs, program management directives, policies and procedures on commonality, and other documents bearing on the issue. In addition, we discussed with program officials the history and future plans for each jammer as well as reasons for not pursuing commonality.

To determine what efforts the services were undertaking to achieve commonality, we met with officials representing the Joint Electronic Warfare Center and the Joint Coordinating Group for Electronic Warfare. We also met with DOD officials to assess DOD's efforts toward achieving commonality. In addition, we analyzed past and current electronic warfare master plans to determine their effect on commonality.

We performed our work at DOD, Air Force, and Navy organizations responsible for the acquisition of electronic warfare jammers. Primary among these were

- Office of the Under Secretary of Defense (Acquisition), Washington, D.C.;
- Joint Electronic Warfare Center, Kelly Air Force Base, Texas;
- Warner Robins Air Logistics Center, Robins Air Force Base, Georgia;
- Air Force Systems Command, Aeronautical Systems Division, Wright Patterson Air Force Base, Ohio; and
- Naval Air Systems Command, Washington, D.C.

We conducted our review in accordance with generally accepted government auditing standards from June 1990 to June 1991.

Chapter 2

Radar Jammer Commonality Still Not Achieved

Despite long-standing congressional committee emphasis as well as more recent legislation on the need to increase commonality in radar jammers and DOD's stated commitment to commonality, the military services have not taken advantage of opportunities to reduce system proliferation. Instead of realizing the potential cost savings associated with common-service programs, the services continue to pursue duplicative jammer programs at a cost exceeding $9 billion and have achieved no system commonality. Further, since our 1985 report, the prospects for achieving commonality have deteriorated. Service plans to acquire new systems and modify existing radar jammers show that little progress is likely in the future. The proliferation continues largely because DOD has not effectively managed jammer programs to achieve commonality.

Congress Continues to Express Interest in Limiting Electronic Warfare Programs

Congress has had a long-standing interest in reducing proliferation of electronic warfare systems. By urging development of common systems, Congress expects to reduce the costly proliferation of duplicative systems and achieve cost savings in program development, production, and logistics. The following examples illustrate congressional efforts to reduce electronic warfare system proliferation.

The House Conference Report on the National Defense Authorization Act for Fiscal Year 1985 stated:

"The conferees agreed that better coordination is required among all four services in identifying electronic warfare requirements and the programs required to address them. The conferees agreed that greater commonality could be achieved to reduce costs and improve capability.... Accordingly, the conferees request the Secretary of Defense require the services to develop a comprehensive, coordinated electronic warfare plan that addresses...the prospects for commonality and joint systems...."

A 1987 report of the House Committee on Government Operations concerning electronic warfare programs stated:

"This committee has long urged an end to wasteful proliferation in military service production programs. We have particularly emphasized the need to avoid duplication...improve the readiness of our forces, and reduce costs by developing common systems that would meet interservice needs." [Furthermore,] "...increased use of common weapon systems would significantly reduce costs and enhance readiness, interoperability, and reliability."

The House Conference Report on the National Defense Authorization Act for Fiscal Year 1989 stated:

"Further, the conferees direct, as a matter of DOD policy, that when common requirements exist and potential cost savings can be quantified, commonality be maximized to the extent possible in all electronic warfare acquisitions."

The House Conference Report on the National Defense Authorization Act for Fiscal Year 1991 expressed congressional frustration with the management of electronic warfare programs. As a result, the act consolidated selected electronic warfare programs and directed the Under Secretary of Defense for Acquisition to establish a cost-effective joint electronic warfare program for jammers to eliminate redundancy, maximize commonality, and meet operational requirements.

DOD Policies Consider Commonality

DOD agrees on the need for commonality, and its policy statements reflect congressional concerns about electronic warfare system proliferation. DOD policy states that prior to initiating a new acquisition program, the services must consider using or modifying an existing system or initiate a new joint-service development program. DOD policy also requires the services to consider commonality alternatives at various points in the acquisition process.

Common Systems Can Result in Savings

In addition to avoiding unnecessary costs that result from funding a multitude of similar development programs, increased commonality among the services' systems can result in economy of scale savings. For example, the larger quantity buys stemming from common use usually result in lower procurement costs. Similarly, lower support costs result from a more simplified logistics system providing common repair parts, maintenance, test equipment, and training.

Services Continue to Proliferate Costly Jammer Systems

The Air Force and the Navy continue to use, procure, or upgrade 12 different self-protection jammer systems and two different mission support jammer systems for tactical aircraft at an estimated cost exceeding $9 billion. No system commonality has been achieved. Table 2.1 shows the services' current radar jammer systems for tactical fighter and attack aircraft and their costs. These jammers existed in 1985, although some were in a different acquisition phase. For example, the Air Force's ALQ-131 Block II was in production in 1985; whereas, production has now been completed, and an upgrade program is pending. Since 1985, one jammer program, the ALQ-189, has been terminated as discussed on page 19. Another, the ALQ-135 Quick Reaction Capability, was procured at a cost of $256 million and deployed in 1988 but was retired from service in 1991 after Operation Desert Storm. None of the jammers were common to both Air Force and Navy aircraft in 1985 and still are not.

Table 2.1 Current Radar Jammers for Tactical Aircraft

System	User	Phase	Estimated cost (millions)
Self-Protection			
ASPJ	Navy	In production; deployment pending	$2,100
ALQ-101	Air Force	Production complete; to be retired	Unknown
ALQ-119	Air Force	Being upgraded to ALQ-184	Unknown
ALQ-126A	Navy	Production complete; to be retired	Unknown
ALQ-126B	Navy	Production complete	$462
ALQ-131 Block I	Air Force	Production complete; to be retired	$665
ALQ-131 Block II	Air Force	Upgrade pending	$792
ALQ-135 Basic	Air Force	Production complete	Unknown
ALQ-135 Preplanned Product Improvement	Air Force	In production	$1,904
ALQ-137	Air Force	In production	$95
ALQ-164	Marines	In production	$62
ALQ-184	Air Force	In production, upgrade pending	$1,034
Mission Support			
ALQ-99	Air Force	Being upgraded	$726
ALQ-99	Navy/Marine	Being upgraded	$1,263
Total			**$9,103**

Air Force pod jammers illustrate how jammer proliferation has occurred and is continuing. First, the Air Force developed the ALQ-131 Block I in the 1970s to replace the older ALQ-119. While acquiring the ALQ-131 Block I in 1982, the Air Force decided to retain and upgrade the ALQ-119. The upgraded version became known as the ALQ-184. Later, in 1983, the Air Force decided to develop a follow-on version of the ALQ-131 Block I, which was designated the Block II. In 1989, after acquiring over 400 ALQ-131 Block II jammers and 326 ALQ-184 jammers, the Air Force selected the ALQ-184 to meet its future pod jammer needs. Nevertheless, the Air Force now has a requirement to further upgrade both the ALQ-131 Block II and the ALQ-184.

Prospects for Commonality Have Deteriorated

In addition to the continuing proliferation, the potential that existed in 1985 for achieving commonality has deteriorated. Since our 1985 report and DOD's related response that significant commonality was expected to be achieved over the next 10 years, systems having promise for common-service use have become or are becoming service unique.

ASPJ Is Now Navy Unique

Although ASPJ was designated by DOD to be the common jammer of the future, decisions regarding the program resulted in duplicative development costs and higher ASPJ unit production costs. The Navy and the Air Force intended to procure ASPJ systems for use on Navy A-6E, F-14, F/A-18, and AV-8B and Air Force F-16 aircraft. Also, in 1985, the Air Force considered replacing older jammers on its F-111 aircraft with ASPJ. Despite the potential savings of using a common jammer system, DOD rejected ASPJ and decided that the Air Force would develop the ALQ-189, an upgrade of the ALQ-137, at an estimated cost of $637 million. However, after spending $87 million to develop the ALQ-189 program, the Air Force terminated the program because of its high cost. The Air Force continues to produce the ALQ-137 jammer system for the F-111 aircraft.

In 1990, the Air Force withdrew from the ASPJ program, citing poor test results, congressional restrictions on full-rate production, and high cost as the reasons. However, the Air Force still has a requirement for an internal jammer like ASPJ for its F-16 aircraft.

The Air Force's withdrawal resulted in a decrease of 1,499 jammers, or 66 percent of the total program requirement. The withdrawal also contributed toward an increased ASPJ unit cost from an estimated $1.4 million in 1989 to $2.3 million in 1991 for a basic system.

Separate ALQ-99E Upgrades Mean Further Commonality Reduction

The Air Force adopted the Navy's ALQ-99 mission-support jammer in 1974, and the Navy has modified its system several times since then. Currently, the Navy and the Air Force have major upgrade programs underway on the system. The Navy's estimated $1.3 billion upgrade program is to improve the system's receiver components for Navy systems only. In contrast, the Air Force's $726 million upgrade program is aimed at improving the system's multiple transmitters and other components. Only one of the upgraded transmitters will be used by both services. As a result, commonality between the two systems will be further reduced.

DOD Has Not Effectively Managed Jammer Programs to Achieve Commonality

While recognizing the economic savings and operational benefits that could be derived from using a common jammer, DOD has not taken a strong role in the oversight of jammer upgrade programs. According to the Director of Electronic Combat for Tactical Warfare Programs, DOD considers jammer upgrade programs to be minor programs as opposed to acquisition of new systems. Thus, DOD has left the responsibility for managing jammer upgrades to the services. Further, DOD has not effectively developed the 1985 congressionally directed electronic warfare plan to use as an effective tool to achieve commonality.

DOD Lacks Adequate Control Over Service Programs

DOD is responsible for overseeing and managing jammer and other electronic warfare systems. However, DOD does not have the internal controls to manage jammer programs adequately. Such controls could reduce jammer proliferation. An example that illustrates the lack of internal controls involves major upgrades of the ALQ-135.

In 1985, DOD missed attaining potential commonality benefits by not directing the Air Force to evaluate the use of the ALQ-135 and ASPJ on F-15 aircraft. At that time, while ASPJ was under development, the Air Force started developing the preplanned product improvement version of the ALQ-135 without any specific approval by DOD. If the Air Force successfully completes the ongoing estimated $1.9 billion program, the ALQ-135 jammer will have a capability similar to ASPJ's planned capability.

After allowing both systems to enter production, DOD compared the systems in 1991 and found that with repackaging, it would have been possible to use ASPJ in place of the improved ALQ-135. According to the Director of Electronic Combat for Tactical Warfare Programs, a comparison of the jammers should have been made before the ALQ-135 product improvement program began. In addition, a comparison of the jammers when the decisions about the upgrade were made, rather than after the systems entered production, could have resulted in a single jammer system.

Similarly, the separate Navy and Air Force upgrades to the ALQ-99, discussed on page 19, represent another lost opportunity for stronger DOD involvement and oversight. DOD did not direct the services to jointly manage their upgrade programs. As a result, the services are updating two separate parts of the jammer, thereby further reducing its commonality.

Electronic Warfare Master Plan Is Not a Road Map to Commonality

In an effort to achieve greater commonality and reduce cost, conferees on the fiscal year 1986 National Defense Authorization Act, in 1985, directed DOD to develop a detailed master plan for electronic warfare programs. In 1987, Congress further required that the plan describe joint electronic warfare programs that will satisfy requirements against the current and future threat and identify those electronic warfare systems that will be terminated. One of the plan's original goals, as envisioned by DOD, was to provide a road map to electronic warfare system commonality. However, the plan is simply a listing of systems the services plan to acquire or upgrade and contains no provisions for achieving commonality.

Conclusions and Recommendations

The services have demonstrated continued preference for service-unique systems over joint-service systems, thereby not achieving savings possible through a common system. Despite DOD's stated commitment to achieving commonality, it has allowed the services to continue acquiring and upgrading service-unique systems. Thus, a stronger role by DOD in managing jammer programs appears essential if proliferation is to be curtailed.

We therefore recommend that the Secretary of Defense perform an analysis to determine the most cost-effective self-protection jammer for maximum common use on existing Air Force and Navy tactical aircraft. This analysis should weigh each jammer against all other jammers to identify the jammer that provides the highest level of aircraft protection for the funds invested. Costs considered in the analysis should include all future costs applicable to each jammer's life cycle. After the best jammer is selected, DOD could restructure the electronic warfare master plan to prescribe guidance, including timetables, for installing the jammer on the maximum practical number of Air Force and Navy aircraft. This approach should minimize upgrading of the numerous existing jammers.

Until commonality is achieved through implementing the preceding recommendation, we also recommend that the Secretary establish controls over the services' jammer programs, such as DOD review and approval authority, to achieve commonality whenever feasible.

In addition, we recommend that the Secretary require the Air Force and the Navy to merge the separate ALQ-99 upgrade programs into one program to improve commonality.

Matters for Congressional Consideration

Despite long-standing congressional committee emphasis and more recent legislation aimed at promoting commonality, none has been achieved. The potential for commonality that existed in the mid-1980s has since deteriorated. Thus, Congress may want to

- restrict or deny funds to procure new systems or upgrade existing jammers until DOD has done an acceptable analysis consistent with our recommendation to the Secretary of Defense and then fund only those programs that are consistent with the analysis and
- require DOD to establish a joint jammer program office and centrally control all jammer funding to promote commonality.

Congress should also recognize that the scope of our work excluded any jammers that could be under development for future generation aircraft, such as the Advanced Tactical Fighter. Thus, Congress may want to monitor those programs to assure that they do not lead to further jammer proliferation.

Comments From the Department of Defense

DIRECTOR OF DEFENSE RESEARCH AND ENGINEERING

WASHINGTON, DC 20301-3010

3 1 OCT 1991

Mr. Frank C. Conahan
Assistant Comptroller General
National Security and International
   Affairs Division
U. S. General Accounting Office
Washington, DC 20548

Dear Mr. Conahan:

This is the Department of Defense (DoD) response to the General Accounting Office (GAO) draft report entitled "ELECTRONIC WARFARE: Radar Jammer Proliferation Continues", (GAO Code 395140), OSD Case 8766. The DoD partially concurs with the report.

See comment 1.

The DoD is aware of the advantages of commonality. It is DoD policy that, in those instances where the operational requirements can be achieved, and it is a cost-effective approach, commonality is then implemented. However, commonality solely for the sake of commonality, without the prerequisites of common or similar requirements and operational environment and compatible platform system architecture, is counter productive.

See comment 2.

The inter-Service commonality that was envisioned with the Airborne Self-Protection Jammer unfortunately has not been realized. Due to the decline and projected further decline of the DoD budget, some extremely hard choices had to be made. The Air Force made the difficult decision to withdraw from the joint program because it was no longer affordable with the projected resources. Although commonality was not achieved with the Airborne Self-Protection Jammer, it does not mean that radar

See comment 3.

jammers have proliferated or are proliferating. Since the 1985 GAO review of jammer proliferation, there have been no new radar jammer programs. Of the 15 radar jammers studied in the current GAO review, all but one started development prior to 1985; the sole exception, the ALQ-135 Preplanned Product Improvement, started in 1985. Of the 13 self-protection radar jammers

See comment 4.

discussed in the current report, two are no longer in operational use and four more are being eliminated. These actions will reduce the number from 13 to seven--or about a 50 percent reduction, with attendant reduction in the required operation and support costs.

See comment 5.

As stated, it is DoD policy to foster commonality where it makes sense. The area of radar jammers, as well as other electronic warfare areas, have been and will continue to be, scrutinized to identify programs for joint Service use, as well as multiple applications within a given Service.

The detailed DoD comments on the report findings, recommendations, and suggestions to the Congress are provided in the enclosure.

Sincerely,

Charles E. Adolph
By Direction of the Secretary of Defense

Enclosure
As Stated

GAO DRAFT REPORT - DATED SEPTEMBER 9, 1991
(GAO CODE 395140) OSD CASE 8766

"ELECTRONIC WARFARE: RADAR JAMMER PROLIFERATION CONTINUES"

DEPARTMENT OF DEFENSE COMMENTS

* * * * *

FINDINGS

FINDING A: Electronic Warfare Jammers. The GAO reported four
major self-protection systems that are being acquired or that
have upgrades pending are: (1) the Navy Airborne Self-
Protection Jammer and (2) the Air Force ALQ-135, ALQ-131 and
ALQ-184. The GAO explained that the Airborne Self-Protection
Jammer and ALQ-135 are both mounted inside the aircraft, while
the ALQ-131 and the ALQ-184 are contained in pods, which are
mounted underneath the aircraft fuselage or wing. The GAO also
noted that, in addition, the Airborne Self-Protection Jammer is
being developed in a pod configuration. The GAO also explained
that the ALQ-99 is a mission support jammer used on the Navy
EA-6B and the Air Force EF-111A electronic warfare aircraft.

The GAO referenced a 1985 report (OSD Case 6535), in which it
was asserted that the Air Force had not taken full advantage of
the opportunity to use the jointly developed Airborne Self-
Protection Jammer. The GAO had found that the Air Force had
decreased its planned use of the Airborne Self-Protection Jammer
and was developing upgraded versions of other jammers, such as
the ALQ-131, to meet a common threat. The GAO had recommended
that the Secretary of Defense require an independent assessment
of the ALQ-131 and Airborne Self-Protection Jammer programs to
include their relative cost and performance capabilities. The
GAO also had recommended that, after completing the assessment,
the most cost beneficial system should be developed in pod and
internal versions to satisfy interservice requirements. The GAO
noted that, in response, the DoD recognized both the economic
savings and operational benefits that could potentially be
derived from using a common jammer. The GAO noted, however,
that the DoD did not concur with the recommendation because it
said it had already conducted evaluations of these various
jammers and based on those evaluations it was not possible to
satisfy current or short term requirements with a single jammer
in pod and internal versions. The GAO recalled that, according
to the DoD, significant commonality was not possible
immediately; however, ongoing efforts were expected to achieve
50 percent commonality over the next 10 years. Further, the DoD
had stated that it was developing a Congressionally mandated
electronic warfare plan that would provide the best roadmap to
commonality. (pp. 3-4, pp. 14-22/GAO Draft Report)

Enclosure

Now on pp. 2 and 8-14,

DOD RESPONSE: Partially concur. The GAO statement on radar jammer acquisition is partially correct. The DoD is acquiring the Airborne Self-Protection Jammer for the Navy and the ALQ-135 and ALQ-184 jammers for the Air Force. The ALQ-131 Block II production has ceased as a result of a congressionally mandated 1989 competition, which was won by the ALQ-184. The statement that the ALQ-131 and ALQ-184 have "upgrades pending" is incorrect. Should upgrades for those systems materialize, then the Office of the Secretary of Defense, in its oversight role, will review the upgrades. At that time, the cost and programmatic approach will be evaluated, taking into account elimination of redundancy, maximum commonality and essential operational requirements. Further, the pod version of the Airborne Self Protection Jammer for the AV-8B has been terminated.

FINDING B: Congressional Emphasis and DoD Stated Commitment to Commonality. The GAO reported that Congress has had a longstanding interest in reducing proliferation of electronic warfare systems to reduce the costly proliferation of duplicative systems. The GAO cited a 1987 report of the House Committee on Government Operations concerning electronic warfare programs, as well as language in the Conference Reports on the Defense Authorization Acts, in FY 1985 and FY 1989. The GAO pointed out that the Conference Report on the National Defense Authorization Act for FY 1991 expressed Congressional frustration with the management of electronic warfare programs, and as a result, the Act consolidated selected electronic warfare programs and directed the Under Secretary of Defense for Acquisition to establish a cost-effective joint electronic warfare program for jammers.

The GAO also reported that the DoD agrees on the need for commonality. The GAO noted that DoD policy states that prior to initiating a new acquisition program, the Services must consider using or modifying an existing system, or initiate a new joint-Service development program. The GAO noted that DoD policy also requires the Services to consider commonality alternatives at various points in the acquisition process.

The GAO also reported that, in addition to avoiding unnecessary costs that result from funding a multitude of similar development programs, increased commonality among the Services can also result in economy of scale savings. For example, the GAO observed that larger buys stemming from common use usually result in lower procurement costs, and, similarly, lower support costs result from a more simplified logistics system. (pp. 3-6, pp. 23-25/GAO Draft Report)

DOD RESPONSE: Partially concur. The use of the word "joint" is incorrect. The Fiscal Year 1991 Authorization Conference recommendation was worded as follows. "...the conferees establish a consolidated electronic warfare program under the Under Secretary of Defense for Acquisition and recommend an

See comment 6.

See comment 7.

Now on pp. 2 and 16-17,

See comment 8.

authorization of $161.5 million in fiscal year 1991. The Under
Secretary of Defense for Acquisition shall determine the most
cost-effective modernization plan for electronic warfare that
eliminates redundancy, maximizes commonality, and meets
essential operational requirements all at the resource levels
likely to be available with projected future
budgets...implemented not later than March 1, 1991. From that
point on, the Under Secretary shall ensure that the Service
budgets are consistent with his directives." That direction was
carried out. The words "the conferees establish a consolidated
electronic warfare program" refer to the conference action which
combined the FY 1991 production funds for the Airborne Self
Protection Jammer, ALQ-135 and the ALQ-184.

FINDING C: Services Continue to Proliferate Costly Jammer
Systems. The GAO reported that the Air Force and Navy continue
to use, procure, or upgrade 13 different self-protection jammer
systems and two different mission support jammer systems for
tactical aircraft at an estimated cost exceeding $9 billion.
The GAO held that no system commonality has been achieved.
Table 2.1 of the report shows the Services' current radar jammer
systems for tactical fighter and attack aircraft and their cost.
The GAO observed that these same jammers existed in 1985. The
GAO also observed that none of the jammers were common to both
Air Force and Navy aircraft in 1985 and still are not. The GAO
noted that Air Force pod jammers illustrate how jammer
proliferation has occurred and is continuing. The GAO found,
first that the Air Force developed the ALQ-131 Block I in the
1970's to replace the older ALQ-119. The GAO found that, while
acquiring the ALQ-131 Block I in 1982, the Air Force then
decided to upgrade the ALQ-119 (the ALQ-184). The GAO found,
further that, in 1983, the Air Force decided to develop a
follow-on version of the ALQ-131 Block I (designated Block II).
Finally, the GAO found that, in 1989, after acquiring over 400
ALQ-131 Block II jammers and 326 ALQ-184 jammers, the Air Force
selected the ALQ-184 to meet its future pod jammer needs. The
GAO observed, nevertheless, that the Air Force now has a
requirement to further upgrade both the ALQ-131 Block II and
the ALQ-184.

The GAO concluded that the Services have demonstrated continued
preference for Service-unique systems over joint-service
systems, thereby not achieving savings possible through a common
system. (pp. 5-6, pp. 26-28, p. 33/GAO Draft Report)

DOD RESPONSE: Partially concur. Report Table 2.1 (page 27), is
referenced in this Finding. That table, entitled, "Current
Radar Jammers for Tactical Aircraft," contains some errors. The
Airborne Self Protection Jammer and ALQ-135 Quick Reaction
Capability are not current jammers; "current" meaning in
operational use. The Airborne Self Protection Jammer is not
deployed and the ALQ-135 Quick Reaction Capability is no longer
deployed. A more accurate and useful version of the chart from
a proliferation point of view is proposed (see following page).

Now on pp. 3 and 17-18.

See comment 9.

SUGGESTED TABLE 2.1
CURRENT RADAR JAMMERS FOR TACTICAL AIRCRAFT

SYSTEM	USER	IN USE	IN PROD	UPDATE PENDING	DATE INITIATED	ESTIMATED COST ($M)	COMMENTS
SELF PROTECTION JAMMERS							
ASPJ	USN	NO	YES	YES	1976	2,100	
ALQ-101	USAF	YES	NO	NO	1967	UNKNOWN	PHASING OUT
ALQ-119	USAF	YES	NO	NO	1970	UNKNOWN	PHASING OUT
ALQ-126A	USN	YES	NO	NO	1970	UNKNOWN	PHASING OUT
ALQ-126B	USN	YES	NO	NO	1977	462	
ALQ-131 BLOCK I	USAF	YES	NO	NO	1972	665	PHASING OUT
ALQ-131 BLOCK II	USAF	YES	NO	NO	1982	792	
ALQ-135 BASIC	USAF	YES	NO	NO	1971	UNKNOWN	
ALQ-135 QRC	USAF	NO	NO	NO	1981	256	
ALQ-135 P3I	USAF	YES	YES	NO	1985	1,904	
ALQ-137	USAF	YES	NO	NO	1975	95	
ALQ-164	USMC	YES	NO	NO	1980	62	
ALQ-184	USAF	YES	YES	NO	1977	1,034	
SUPPORT JAMMERS							
ALQ-99	USAF	YES	NO	YES	1974	726	
ALQ-99	USN	YES	NO	YES	1969	1,263	
TOTAL						9,359	

See comment 10.

See comment 11.

A key element in the proposed chart is that there is no upgrade to either the ALQ-131 Block II or the ALQ-184. Not evident in the GAO chart is the imminent retirement of the ALQ-101 and ALQ-119 and the future retirement of the ALQ-126A and ALQ-131 Block I. Of the 13 self-protection jammers listed, four are being phased out, only three are in production, and only one of the three has a planned update. Thus, the current number of jammers are lower than those reflected in the GAO chart and the total number is decreasing.

FINDING D: Prospects for Commonality Have Deteriorated. The GAO reported that, in addition to continuing proliferation, the potential that existed in 1985 for achieving commonality has deteriorated. The GAO observed that, since its 1985 report, systems having promise for common-service use have become or are becoming Service unique. The GAO found that, although the Airborne Self-Protection Jammer was designated by DoD to be the common jammer of the future, decisions regarding the program resulted in duplicative development costs and higher Airborne Self-Protection Jammer unit production costs. The GAO found that the Navy and Air Force intended to procure Airborne Self-Protection Jammer systems for use on Navy the A-6E, F-14, F/A-18, AV-8B aircraft and Air Force F-16 aircraft. The GAO also noted that, in 1985, the Air Force considered using the Airborne Self-Protection Jammer to replace older jammers on its F-111 aircraft. The GAO observed, however, that despite the potential savings of using a common jammer system, the DoD rejected the Airborne Self-Protection Jammer and decided that the Air Force would develop the ALQ-189, an upgrade of the ALQ-137, at an estimated cost of $637 million. The GAO found, however, that after spending $87 million to develop the ALQ-189 program, the Air Force terminated the program because of its high cost, and instead continues to produce the ALQ-137.

The GAO further reported that, early in 1990, the Air Force withdrew from the Airborne Self-Protection Jammer program entirely--citing as the reasons: (1) poor test results, (2) Congressional restrictions on full-rate production, and (3) high cost. The GAO found that the Air Force withdrawal resulted in a decrease of 1,499 jammers or 66 percent of the total program requirement. In addition, the GAO found that the withdrawal contributed toward an increased unit cost from an estimated $1.4 million in 1989 to $2.3 million in 1991 for a basic system.

Finally, the GAO reported that the Air Force adopted the Navy ALQ-99 mission-support jammer in 1974, and the Navy modified its system several times since then. The GAO found that the Navy and Air Force have major upgrade programs underway on that system. The GAO noted that the Navy's estimated $1.3 billion upgrade program is aimed at improving the system receiver components for Navy systems only, and the Air Force $726 million upgrade program is aimed at improving the multiple transmitters and other system components. The GAO reported that only one of

the upgraded transmitters will be used by both Services--thus,
commonality between the two systems will be further reduced.
The GAO concluded that, despite longstanding Congressional
emphasis and legislation aimed at promoting commonality, none
has been achieved. The GAO further concluded that the potential
for commonality that existed in the mid-1980s has since
deteriorated. (pp. 6-7, pp. 28-30, p. 34/GAO Draft Report)

Now on pp. 3 and 19.

See comment 12.

DOD RESPONSE: Partially concur. In general, the prospects for
commonality in Electronic Warfare systems have improved. The
DoD acknowledges a self-protection commonality opportunity loss
in the Airborne Self Protection Jammer program. However, there
are common electronic warfare programs, such as the ALE-47 chaff
and flare dispenser, the AAR-47 missile warning system, the
ALQ-156 missile warning system, and the ALQ-99 Band 9/10
transmitter. These have occurred since 1985, and have been
influenced by the DoD Electronic Warfare Plan.

See comment 13.

The GAO provided an incomplete picture of the decision to equip
the F-111 aircraft with a self-protection jamming capability.
The ALQ-94, which was the self-protection jammer on the F-111A,
D, E, and F aircraft, became logistically unsupportable. The
Air Force evaluated the ALQ-189 and Airborne Self-Protection
Jammer as a replacement for the ALQ-94. The life cycle cost
difference between the two systems was insignificant.
Therefore, the Air Force conducted an open competition, and the
ALQ-189 and the Airborne Self Protection Jammer contractors
submitted proposals. As a result of the proposals, the Air
Force determined that neither system was affordable. The Air
Force then elected to use the existing ALQ-137, the self-
protection jammer for the bomber and electronic warfare versions
of the F-111, as the replacement jammer for the ALQ-94. Thus,
the ALQ-94 is being phased out of the inventory. Installation
of the ALQ-137 in the F-111 aircraft has been completed, and
deliveries of ALQ-137 spares will be completed in November 1991.

See comment 14.

The GAO reported that the Air Force withdrew from the Airborne
Self-Protection Jammer program "...citing poor test results,
congressional restrictions on full-rate production, and high
cost as the reasons." A perspective of the times is necessary
for a complete understanding of the Air Force withdrawal from
the program. The Berlin wall had just fallen. There was a
ground swell for a "peace dividend". The Air Force as well as
the other services, was directed to find three billion dollars
each across the then-current Five Year Defense Plan to
contribute to the "peace dividend". The Air Force had to
sacrifice some of its programs to meet this mandated reduction.
In a memorandum to a congressional staff member, the Director,
Electronic and Special Programs, Office of the Assistant
Secretary (Acquisition), stated "The Air Force terminated the
Airborne Self Protection Jammer program due to affordability".
The "poor test results" cited by the GAO constitute a factor in
the affordability decision. The test results were associated
with prototype models of the Airborne Self Protection Jammer.

The deficiencies experienced by these models were being corrected in the production verification models. For the Air Force to continue in the program would have required an investment of several million production dollars prior to testing of the redesigned system. Given the budget reduction climate, the Air Force was unwilling to make that investment. The Navy, however, chose to continue with the ASPJ program.

See comment 15.

The GAO is critical of the Air Force and the Navy for a lack of commonality between their versions of the ALQ-99 carried on Navy EA-6Bs and Air Force EF-111As. To achieve commonality, three basic elements are essential. First, a common mission requirement; second, a common operational employment; and third, a common platform architecture and support structure. While Navy and Air Force mission requirements and the operational function for the EA-6B and EF-111A resemble each other, the operational environment and platforms are substantially different. The EA-6B is a carrier based aircraft with the receiver portion of its prime mission equipment carried internally and the transmitters carried externally in pods. The EF-111A is a supersonic land-based aircraft with both the transmitters and receivers carried internally. The EA-6B mission includes escort jamming, standoff jamming, communications jamming, and shipboard defensive jamming along with hard-kill defense suppression through the use of High Speed Antiradiation Missiles (HARM). The primary mission of the EF-111A is standoff jamming against radars. The EA-6B carries a pilot and three operators. The EF-111A carries a crew of one pilot and one electronic warfare officer. The EA-6B and EF-111A platforms are drastically different, however, their receivers are 10 to 12 percent common and the following levels of transmitter commonality have been achieved at the shop replaceable assembly or the module level.

See comment 16.

Transmitter Band	Percent Common	Commonality Basis
4	75	SRU
5/6	58	SRU
7	58	SRU
8	67	SRU
9/10	80	Module

FINDING E: The DoD Lacks Adequate Controls Over Service Programs. The GAO reported that the DoD has not effectively exercised oversight over jammer upgrade programs--thus, resulting in jammer proliferation. The GAO noted that the Director of Electronic Combat for Tactical Warfare Programs considers jammer upgrade programs to be minor programs, as opposed to acquisition of completely new systems. The GAO found that, therefore, the DoD has left the responsibility for managing jammer upgrades to the Services. The GAO also concluded that, while the DoD is responsible for overseeing and managing jammer and other electronic warfare systems, it does not have the internal controls to manage jammer programs effectively. For example, the GAO noted that, while the Airborne Self-Protection Jammer was under development and without any specific approval by the DoD, the Air Force began two upgrades of its ALQ-135 jammer: The first upgrade cost $256 million, and the second is estimated to cost $1.9 billion. The GAO reported that the DoD compared systems in 1991 and found that, with repackaging, it would have been possible to use the Airborne Self-Protection Jammer in place of the improved ALQ-135. The GAO further reported that, according to the Director of Electronic Combat for Tactical Warfare Programs, a comparison of jammers should have been made before the ALQ-135 product improvement program began. The GAO concluded that a comparison of the jammers when the decisions about the upgrades were made could have resulted in a single common system.

The GAO also reported that the separate Navy and Air Force upgrades to the ALQ-99 represent another lost opportunity for stronger DoD involvement and oversight. The GAO observed that the DoD did not direct the Services to manage their upgrade programs jointly. In addition, the GAO reported that the DoD has not developed the Congressionally mandated Electronic Warfare Master Plan so that it can be used as a tool or roadmap to achieve commonality. The GAO found the plan reflects little more than listings of systems that the Services plan to acquire or upgrade and contains no provisions for achieving commonality.

The GAO concluded that, despite the DoD stated commitment to achieving commonality, it has allowed the Services to continue acquiring and upgrading Service-unique systems--thus, a stronger role by the DoD in managing jammer programs appears essential if proliferation is to be curtailed. (pp. 7-8, pp. 30-33/GAO Draft Report)

Now on pp. 4 and 19-20.

DOD RESPONSE: Partially concur. The GAO criticizes the Director of Electronic Combat for considering "...jammer programs to be minor programs, as opposed to acquisition of completely new systems." The designation of major or nonmajor (using nonmajor and minor as synonymous) programs has its basis in law (Title 10 U.S. Code Section 2430) and is promulgated in DoD Instruction 5000.2. A major program is one that is estimated by the Under Secretary of Defense for Acquisition to require:

See comment 17.

- an eventual total expenditure for research, development, test, and evaluation of more than $200 million in fiscal year 1980 constant dollars (approximately $300 million in fiscal year 1990 constant dollars), or

- an eventual total expenditure for procurement of more than $1 billion in fiscal year 1980 constant dollars (approximately $1.8 billion in fiscal year 1990 constant dollars).

All other programs are nonmajor (minor) programs. The Service
Acquisition Executives exercise direction of nonmajor programs
and delegated major programs. When required, the Defense
Acquisition Executive can direct common approaches in nonmajor
programs. Currently, the Conventional Systems Committee is
reviewing missile warning systems with the expectation of
directing common approaches. The most cost effective
approaches will be used.

See comment 18.

The GAO states "...that the DoD has not developed the
congressionally mandated Electronic Warfare Master Plan so that
it can be used as a tool or roadmap to achieve commonality."
Annually, the DoD submits to the Congress numerous reports and
plans. Recently, the Congress presented the DoD with a list of
documents it will no longer require. The DoD Electronic Warfare
Plan was not on that list, the message being that the DoD
Electronic Warfare Plan is serving a useful purpose. The DoD
Electronic Warfare Plan is not directive in nature. However, it
does lay out clearly how anticipated advances in technology and
predicted changes in force structures will meld to produce
substantial decreases in numbers and types of systems currently
employed in aircraft self-protection. The DoD Electronic
Warfare Plan is the only comprehensive document that contains
the electronic combat programs for the Military Services; from
technology, engineering and manufacturing development,
production, and inventory. Contrary to GAO opinion, it is the
DoD view that the plan does provide a tool for achieving
commonality. It is the only document that provides inter-
Service visibility into the electronic combat programs--thereby
(1) making redundancy obvious, (2) identifying possible
opportunities for commonality, and (3) eliminating duplication.
The force structure appendix provides a measure of the DoD
progress in eliminating duplicative or redundant programs.
Examples of joint use systems fostered by the Plan are the
AAR-47, the AVR-2, the ALQ-156, the ALE-47, and the ALQ-99
Band 9/10 transmitter.

*****
RECOMMENDATIONS

RECOMMENDATION 1: The GAO recommended that the Secretary of
Defense perform an analysis to determine the most cost-effective
self-protection jammer for maximum common use on existing Air
Force and Navy tactical aircraft. (The GAO specified that the
analysis should weigh each jammer against all other jammers to
identify the jammer that provides the highest level of aircraft
protection for the funds invested. The GAO also stipulated that
costs considered in the analysis should include all future costs
applicable to each system's life cycle.) (p. 33/GAO Draft
Report)

Now on pp. 4 and 21.

See comment 19.

DOD RESPONSE: Concur. The DoD already has accomplished the
suggested analysis as part of the congressionally-directed
Defense Acquisition Board review of electronic warfare programs

held in February 1991. The Defense Acquisition Board findings
were presented to the Congress and briefed to selected
congressional staff members. Commonality, while a laudable goal
in many programs, does not always result in the lowest cost or
most cost effective program.

RECOMMENDATION 2: The GAO recommended that, after the best
jammer is selected, the Secretary of Defense restructure the
Electronic Warfare Master Plan to prescribe guidance, including
timetables, for installing the jammer on Air Force and Navy
aircraft in lieu of upgrade programs for existing jammers.
(p. 33/GAO Draft Report)

Now on pp. 4 and 21.

See comment 20.

DOD RESPONSE: Nonconcur. Based on the Congressionally
requested Defense Acquisition Board review held in February
1991, the DoD is embarked on the most cost-effective road to
modern aircraft self-protection.

RECOMMENDATION 3: The GAO recommended that, until commonality
is achieved through implementing the preceding recommendation,
the Secretary of Defense establish controls over the jammer
programs of the Military Services--such as DoD review and
approval authority--to achieve commonality whenever feasible.
(pp. 33-34/GAO Draft Report)

Now on pp. 4 and 21.

See comment 21.

DOD RESPONSE: Concur. The recommended controls currently
exist. The Office of the Secretary of Defense has oversight
over Service programs. That oversight begins in the Planning,
Programming, and Budgeting System and construction of the
Program Objectives Memorandum every other year. The Service
inputs are subject to substantial scrutiny during the process.
Annually, the Service inputs to the President's Budget are
reviewed and adjusted in the DoD Comptroller Budget Review.
Programs may be eliminated or have their funding adjusted as a
result of the process. Further, the Under Secretary of Defense
for Acquisition may elect to withhold money from Service
programs. That option provides a forcing function over any
Service program needing management attention. For FY 1992,
money has been withheld from both Air Force and Navy missile
warning programs until the Services report their plans for a
common approach to missile warning acquisition programs to the
Conventional Systems Committee. The Military Services are,
thus, forced to comply with the intent that the maximum feasible
commonality be achieved in the missile warning area consistent
with meeting operational requirements, affordability, and cost
effectiveness.

RECOMMENDATION 4: The GAO recommended that the Secretary of
Defense require the Air Force and the Navy to merge the separate
ALQ-99 upgrade programs into one program to improve commonality.
(p. 34/GAO Draft Report)

Now on pp. 4 and 21.

See comment 22.

DOD RESPONSE: Nonconcur. Appropriate action has been taken.
The Navy and Air Force offices responsible for the development

of the ALQ-99 have signed a document titled "Memorandum of
Agreement Between the United States Naval Air Systems Command
(PMA 234) And the United States Air Force (USAF) Aeronautical
Systems Division (ASD) Directorate of Electronic Combat
(ASD/RWW) On the Establishment of Cooperative Efforts Relating
to the United States Navy (USN)/EA-6B and the USAF/EF-111A
System Improvement Program (SIP) Tactical Jamming System (TJS)."
While the two platforms are very different, the substantial
effort dedicated to commonality in this program has resulted in
a high degree of commonality in the ALQ-99 transmitters.
Physical constraints and crew limitations have precluded a high
degree of commonality within the receiver systems.

MATTERS FOR CONGRESSIONAL CONSIDERATION

SUGGESTION 1: The GAO suggested that the Congress restrict or
deny funds to procure new or upgrade existing jammers until the
DoD has done an acceptable analysis, consistent with the GAO
recommendation to the Secretary of Defense--and then fund only
those programs that are (a) consistent with the analyses, and
(b) require the DoD to establish a joint jammer program office
and centrally control all jammer funding to promote commonality.

See comment 23.

DOD RESPONSE: Partially concur. The DoD has completed and
informed the Congress of the findings of a congressionally
directed Defense Acquisition Board review of self-protection
jammer effectiveness and commonality issues. Joint program
offices will be established when and if such an organizational
structure is warranted.

SUGGESTION 2: The GAO suggested that the Congress recognize
that the scope of the GAO work excluded any jammers that could
be under development for future generation aircraft, such as the
Advanced Tactical Fighter--thus Congress may want to require
properly authorized personnel to examine those programs to
assure that they do not lead to further proliferation of

Now on pp. 5 and 22.

jammers. (pp.34-35/GAO Draft Report)

DOD RESPONSE: (Defer to the Congress)

The following are GAO's comments on the Department of Defense's letter dated October 31, 1991.

GAO Comments

1. We disagree that the Department of Defense (DOD) implements commonality when it is cost-effective and can achieve operational requirements. While acquiring the self-protection jammers discussed in this report, DOD missed numerous opportunities to achieve commonality, even though Air Force and Navy tactical aircraft face a common threat and have common operational requirements for jammers to provide protection against that threat. For example, as early as 1982, an Air Force official pointed out the opportunity to standardize jammers for the F-15, F-16, and F-111 aircraft, thereby avoiding the duplicative costs of upgrading three different jammers. Nevertheless, separate jammer developments were allowed to proceed.

2. The Air Force's stated reason for withdrawing from the ASPJ program because of its affordability is contradicted by some of its own actions. For example, when the Air Force withdrew from the ASPJ program, it did not cancel its requirement for an internal jammer like ASPJ for its F-16 aircraft. This requirement still exists today. In addition, it procured the ALQ-135 Quick Reaction Capability jammer for the F-15 in the past at a unit cost of $3.9 million and is currently procuring the ALQ-135 Preplanned Product Improvement jammer for the F-15 at a unit cost of $2.6 million. Both jammers were more expensive than the ASPJ's estimated unit cost of $1.4 million at the time the Air Force withdrew from the program.

3. On page 17, we state that the same jammers existed in 1985, although some were in a different acquisition phase. Since our 1985 report, no new jammer programs have been started, with the possible exception of jammers for future generation aircraft. However, the services have continued proliferation through the development, production, and/or modification of several jammers, all to protect the same type of aircraft against the same threat. These include the ASPJ, ALQ-126B, ALQ-131 Block II, ALQ-135 Quick Reaction Capability, ALQ-135 Preplanned Product Improvement, ALQ-137, ALQ-164, ALQ-184, and ALQ-189. In addition, both the Air Force and the Navy are modifying versions of the ALQ-99.

4. DOD's recount of the self-protection jammers is in error. Only one, the ALQ-135 Quick Reaction Capability, has been withdrawn from service. In addition, the ALQ-101, ALQ-126A, and ALQ-131 Block I are scheduled to be withdrawn. The ALQ-119 is being modified and redesignated the ALQ-184. However, the reduction will likely be largely offset by pending

upgrades to the ASPJ, ALQ-131 Block II, and ALQ-184. In addition, the ALQ-126B jammer, which is in need of upgrading, is not to be replaced by ASPJ. Thus, this jammer will likely be upgraded to enable it to meet Navy requirements.

5. See comment 1.

6. While production has ceased on the ALQ-131 Block II jammer, the Air Force has approved, but not yet funded, upgrade programs for both it and the ALQ-184 to enable those jammers to meet operational requirements.

7. The ASPJ pod program was terminated after our audit work was completed. We therefore changed the report to reflect the termination.

8. Section 182 (c) of the National Defense Authorization Act for Fiscal Year 1991 states:

"The Under Secretary of Defense for Acquisition shall establish an affordable, cost-effective, joint electronic warfare modernization program for the Air Force and Navy that eliminates redundancy among the programs ... maximizes commonality among those programs, and meets essential operational requirements." (Underscoring supplied.)

9. Table 2.1 accurately depicts that ASPJ is in production. We modified the table to indicate that the system has not yet been deployed. The ALQ-135 Quick Reaction Capability jammers were deployed in 1988; however, most were not installed due to reliability and other problems. Some of the jammers were used in 1991 during Operation Desert Storm and have since been discarded. We therefore deleted it from table 2.1.

10. See comment 6.

11. We modified table 2.1 to reflect the planned retirements of the ALQ-101, ALQ-126A, and ALQ-131 Block I. The ALQ-119 is not being retired; it is being upgraded to the ALQ-184 model as shown in table 2.1. Also see comments 4 and 6.

12. Missile warning systems and chaff and flare dispensers were not the subject of our review. Our report deals only with jammers and shows that commonality has not improved.

13. DOD's explanation of the decision does not reveal that DOD first spent $87 million trying to develop the ALQ-189 for the F-111 before terminating the program in 1987. At the same time, ASPJ was being developed. This is

an example of unnecessary development costs that result from not achieving common systems. We therefore did not change our report.

14. See comment 2.

15. The differences in the EA-6B and EF-111A cited in DOD's explanation do not preclude commonality of the ALQ-99. The only element of the three mentioned by DOD that is absolutely essential for achieving commonality is a common mission requirement. Both the EA-6B and the EF-111 share a primary mission of stand-off jamming. The other missions assigned to the EA-6B have no impact on the degree of commonality possible. The EA-6B also has a communications jamming mission and is equipped with a separate jammer for that mission.

16. We recognize the existing commonality between the two versions of the ALQ-99. However, the commonality that existed when the Air Force originally adopted the Navy version has since diminished because of separately managed modification programs. Our concern is that the existing commonality will be further diminished because of the major modification programs being pursued by the Air Force and the Navy. For example, under the current upgrade programs, only one of the jammer's several transmitters is being acquired jointly.

17. DOD has left responsibility for managing the jammer upgrades to the services because the upgrades are considered minor programs. The definitions of major and nonmajor programs notwithstanding, DOD has the authority to manage these programs if it chooses. Because the services have demonstrated a continued preference for service-unique systems, achieving common-service systems appears unlikely without a stronger role by DOD in managing the programs.

18. Our report does not state that the electronic warfare master plan serves no useful purpose. While the plan does provide visibility of service electronic warfare programs, it contains no provisions for achieving commonality and is not a commonality plan or roadmap.

19. The Defense Acquisition Board's review of electronic warfare programs and the related analysis is the subject of an ongoing GAO assignment. Our review to date indicates that DOD's analysis did not attempt to determine the most cost-effective, self-protection jammer for maximum common use and that the analysis did not address the objective of our recommendation.

20. See comment 19.

21. While the controls cited by DOD do exist, we believe our report demonstrates that they have not been effective in achieving commonality.

22. The provisions of the agreement cited by DOD will not assure that the maximum practical degree of commonality will be achieved. Only one of the jammer's several transmitters is to be modified jointly. Other components will be upgraded separately by the services. See comments 15 and 16.

23. See comment 19.

Major Contributors to This Report

National Security and International Affairs Division, Washington, D.C.

Charles A. Ward, Evaluator

Atlanta Regional Office

Jackie B. Guin, Assistant Director
Allan C. Richardson, Evaluator-in-Charge
Danny G. Owens, Site Senior
Wendy G. Piggott, Evaluator
Jose A. Ramos, Evaluator

United States
General Accounting Office
Washington, D.C. 20548

Official Business
Penalty for Private Use $300